The Churches of

Broad Way

(The Cults)

By Rod Durost

Introduction

In self reflection one day, I realized that in trying to be a Christian I was not doing all that I could to lead others to Christ. There was my next door neighbor, a family in town who were our friends, and their family members who had not heard the good news.

I envisioned myself standing at the judgment seat of The Master and hanging my head in shame because I had not told these people the truth. Telling my wife, Brother David & Sister Christine, that I was ashamed was my first step toward doing God's will.

My neighbor & our family friends were Catholics and thought they knew the truth. Therefore, I set out to find all I could on Catholicism. The first book that I read also dealt with several other sects and as I became more involved, I felt God telling me to study the ones that had a cult status to them.

At first I chose three, but a fourth showed up on my door step and I felt compelled to add this one also. After I finished the four manuscripts, I wrote a cover letter and sent the catholic manuscript by mail to my neighbor & our family friends. I then started getting requests for more of this information from a variety of sources and discovered that perhaps what God was telling me to do is to put all this in a book as a reference for others.

I hope as you read this book that you too will realize that we are in a race. God is not going to let this world go on merrily thinking it is in charge of its self. One day it will be all over and the wicked will be judged. Make sure you don't have to hang your head in shame. I expect The Master will say to those who have heard the message of truth and did not believe, "You made your choice."

Romans 14:11 -12

11 For it is written, *As* I live, saith the Lord, every knee shall bow to me, and every tongue shall confess to God.

12 So then every one of us shall give account of himself to God.

Letter To The Reader

Dear Friend,

This book is presented without malice, or presumed feeling of superiority.

Rather, it is presented with compassion and love.

You do not have to believe me or the authors I used to complete this work.

Just ask God for guidance in seeking the truth or error of this book. I will trust God to guide you to the truth.

****

Psalms 71:1 In thee, O LORD, do I put my trust: let me never be put to confusion.

****

In Love & in Christ,

Rod Durost

Table of Contents:

Matt. 7:13 Enter ye in at the strait gate: for wide *is* the gate, and **broad** *is* the **way**, that leadeth to destruction, and many there be which go in there at:

R evelation Churches

Revelation 2:12-29

*The Heretical Church - Pergamos

12 And to the angel of the church in Pergamos write; these things saith he which hath the sharp sword with two edges;

13 I know thy works, and where thou dwellest, *even* where Satan's seat *is:* and thou holdest fast my name, and hast not denied my faith, even in those days wherein Antipas *was* my faithful martyr, who was slain among you, where Satan dwelleth.

14 But I have a few things against thee, because thou hast there them that hold the doctrine of Balaam, who taught Balac to cast a stumbling block before the children of Israel, to eat things sacrificed unto idols, and to commit fornication.

15 So hast thou also them that hold the doctrine of the Nicolaitanes, which thing I hate.

16 Repent; or else I will come unto thee quickly, and will fight against them with the sword of my mouth.

17 He that hath an ear, let him hear what the Spirit saith unto the churches; to him that overcometh will I give to eat of the hidden manna, and will give him a white stone, and in the stone a new name written, which no man knoweth saving he that receiveth *it.*

*Thompson Chain Reference notes

*Church of the False Prophetess - Thyatira

18 And unto the angel of the church in Thyatira write; these things saith the Son of God, who hath his eyes like unto a flame of fire, and his feet *are* like fine brass;

19 I know thy works, and charity, and service, and faith, and thy patience, and thy works; and the last *to be* more than the first.

20 Notwithstanding I have a few things against thee, because thou sufferest that woman Jezebel, which calleth herself a prophetess, to teach and to seduce my servants to commit fornication, and to eat things sacrificed unto idols.

21 And I gave her space to repent of her fornication; and she repented not.

22 Behold, I will cast her into a bed, and them that commit adultery with her into great tribulation, except they repent of their deeds.

23 And I will kill her children with death; and all the churches shall know that I am he which searcheth the reins and hearts: and I will give unto every one of you according to your works.

24 But unto you I say, and unto the rest in Thyatira, as many as have not this doctrine, and which have not known the depths of Satan, as they speak; I will put upon you none other burden.

25 But that which ye have *already* hold fast till I come.

26 And he that overcometh, and keepeth my works unto the end, to him will I give power over the nations:

27 And he shall rule them with a rod of iron; as the vessels of a potter shall they be broken to shivers: even as I received of my Father.

28 And I will give him the morning star.

29 He that hath an ear, let him hear what the Spirit saith unto the churches.

*Thompson Chain Reference notes

Catholicism

The "C" Church

Historically, Revelation 2:12-17, is talking about this church.

Pergamos is this church at the time of Constantine and is also a church supported by the government in modern times.

Thyatira, Revelation 2:18-29 is this church during the apostasy, which during modern times also refers to cults.

~~~~~~~~~~~~~~

According to the dictionary:

Cult - a religion that is considered or held to be false or unorthodox or its members

~~~~~~~~~~~~~~

This cult, "the C Church", enslaves 65 million in the United States according to statistics from USA Today. And according to National Geographic "Inside the Vatican" it enslaves 1 BILLION.

I call this church, as well as the others, cults by the fact that they have left the gospel of Jesus Christ and have gone to pagan or man's beliefs.

Rev. 17:5 And upon her forehead *was* a name written, MYSTERY, BABYLON THE GREAT, THE MOTHER OF HARLOTS AND ABOMINATIONS OF THE EARTH.

ROMAN CATHOLIC TEACHING:

CONCERNING THE BIBLE - C TEACHES:

I. That tradition, apocryphal writings, etc., are to be accepted on a par with the Bible.

THE BIBLE TEACHES:

1. That the Scriptures are alone sufficient (Deut.4:2; ALSO).

> **Isaiah 8:20** To the law and to the testimony: if they speak not according to this word, *it is* because *there is* no light in them.

2. That the commandments of God are made of no effect by the traditions of men (Matt. 15: 3, 6).

3. That those who teach the commandments of men as doctrine worship God in vain (Matt. 15: 9).

4: That there is no redemption in corruptible things received by tradition from the fathers (1 Peter 1:18).

5. That the Scripture is sufficient to make the man of God perfect (2 Tim. 3: 15-17).

6. That there is to be no addition to, or subtraction from the Word of God (Rev. 22: 18, 19).

II. That the Catholic Church only has the right to interpret the Scriptures.

THE BIBLE TEACHES:

1. The Scriptures are for all (John 5:39; Acts17:11; 1 Peter 2:2; 2 Peter 1:19; Rev. 1:3).

2. The Scriptures are NOT to be specially interpreted

> **2Peter 1:20** Knowing this first, that no prophecy of the scripture is of any private interpretation.

III. That they alone have the right Bible.

> NOTE: Why then don't they encourage their members of the congregations to study and search the scriptures for the truth?

∧∧

CONCERNING THE CHURCH - C TEACHES:

I. That the Catholic Church is the only true apostolic church.

THE BIBLE TEACHES:

I. The true church (in the figure of the star crowned woman) went into hiding 1260 days (Rev. 12: 1-7).

NOTE: A day in prophetic history represents a year (Ezek. 4: 5, 6)

2. Catholic Church came into being while; the true church was in hiding

NOTE: There have always been true Christians, but history records them as heretics recorded by Catholic history.

3. The Catholic Church is a union of church and state. There was no union of church and state until Constantine in 325 A. D. so the Catholic Church could not have existed before that date.

4. The church for the first three centuries was called the Church of Christ (Rom. 16: 16), Church of God (1 Cor. 1: 1), Church of the First Born (Heb. 12:23), etc. It was never called the Catholic Church until the time of the apostasy.

5. The Catholic Church is defined as the apostate church in the Scriptures and is called the Mother of Harlots (Rev. 17: 1-18).

(1.) She is a city on seven hills (Rev. 17:9, 18).

NOTE: Rome, the center of Catholicism, is built on seven hills.

(2.) She sits on many waters-peoples, multitudes, nations and tongues (Rev. 17:1, 15).

(3.) She has the world drunk with the wine of her spiritual fornication (Rev. 17:1, 2).

(4.) She is drunk with the blood of martyrs (Rev. 17: 6).

NOTE: Read the history of her inquisitions.

(5.) She is Mysterious (Rev. 17: 5).

NOTE: Has there ever been anything more mysterious than the Catholic Church?

(6.) She is called Babylon (Rev. 17: 5).

NOTE: Babylon means confusion. She is the cause of all spiritual confusion in the world. She changed the name, form of government, act of baptism and is the originator of all human creeds. All these changes have thrown the world into spiritual confusion.

(7.) She is called the "Mother of Harlots."

NOTE: In her catechism she teaches she is the mother of all churches.

(8.) Therefore the Catholic Church is not the only true apostolic church, but she is the APOSTATE church.

II. That Peter founded the church at Rome and that the church is built on him.

THE BIBLE TEACHES:

1. The apostles only had power to confer spiritual gifts (Acts 6: 1-6; Acts 8: 12-18; 19:6, 7; 2 Tim. 1:6).

2. Paul longed to visit the church at Rome in order that he might impart unto them some spiritual gifts (Rom. 1:1O, 11).

NOTE: This shows that the church at Rome was not organized by any apostle or it would have already possessed spiritual gifts.

3. Therefore Peter did not found the church at Rome, for had he done so, having the power of an apostle, he would have conferred spiritual gifts upon the church.

4. Peter denies that the church was built on him (1 Peter 2: 4-6).

5. The church is built on "Petra"-meaning rock. Christ is the ""Petra" or "rock"

> **1Cor. 10:4** And did all drink the same spiritual drink: for they drank of that spiritual Rock that followed them: and that Rock was Christ.

∧∧

THE PAPACY - C TEACHES:

I. That Peter was the first Pope and head of the church.

THE BIBLE TEACHES:

1. Peter denied being head of the church. He said Christ is the head

> **1Peter 2:4-6** To whom coming, *as unto* a living stone, disallowed indeed of men, but chosen of God, *and* precious,

> 5 Ye also, as lively stones, are built up a spiritual house, an holy priesthood, to offer up spiritual sacrifices, acceptable to God by Jesus Christ.

> 6 Wherefore also it is contained in the scripture, Behold, I lay in Zion a chief corner stone, elect, precious: and he that believeth on him shall not be confounded.

2. Paul said Christ is the head of the church (Eph.5:23; Col. 1:18).

3. Peter did not claim superiority (1 Peter 5:1).

4. Even Paul, speaking of himself, said he was not behind the chiefest apostles (2 Cor. 11: 5).

5. James, and not Peter, presided at the first church council (Acts 15: 13, 19)

6. Christ taught the apostles not to exercise dominion over anyone (Matt. 20: 25, 26).

7. First "Papa" or pope mentioned was in the sixth century.

II. That the popes are successors to Peter.

THE BIBLE TEACHES:

1. Only one case of apostolic succession in the Scriptures (Acts 1: 15-26)

2. The successor of an apostle must have accompanied with Christ from the baptism of John to the ascension of Christ (Acts 1: 21, 22).

3. None today, or immediately following the days of the apostles, could meet the requirements of an apostle or the successor of an apostle. Therefore it is scriptural plain that there is to be no apostolic succession.

4. When James was beheaded they did not meet and select one to take his place, as in the case of Judas (Acts 1:21-26)

III. That the pope is the Vicar or representative of Christ on earth.

THE: BIBLE TEACHES:

1. The only personal representative of Christ on earth is the Comforter or Holy Spirit (John 14: 15-17; 26: 16: 7).

NOTE: While all Christians are considered representatives, they are not representatives as is the Holy Spirit.

IV. That the pope is infallible.

THE BIBLE TEACHES:

1. Paul rebuked Peter because he was at fault, therefore Peter was fallible (Gal. 2: 11 - 14).

NOTE: Some Catholics claim that Peter was only infallible in relation to spiritual things; therefore the popes are only infallible in spiritual commands, but not necessarily in morality. It can not be too well noted that Peter was at fault in a spiritual matter.

V. That the popes and priest should live in an unmarried state.

THE BIBLE TEACHES:

1. Peter was married and therefore could not have been a Catholic pope (Matt. 8: 14).

2. Paul said Peter had a wife (I Cor. 9:5)

> **1Timothy 3:2** A bishop then must be blameless, **the husband of one wife,** vigilant, sober, of good behavior, given to hospitality, apt to teach;

VI. That the pope should be called "Holy Lord God, the pope."

THE BIBLE TEACHES:

1. Peter would not have made a good pope, for he would not allow men to worship him (Acts 10: 25, 26).

2. Paul, Peter's equal, would not allow men to worship him (Acts 14: 14, 15).

3. Christ forbade the worshipping of men.

> **Matt. 4:10** Then saith Jesus unto him, Get thee hence, Satan: for it is written, **Thou shalt worship the Lord thy God, and him only shalt thou serve.**

4. Not even an angel is to be worshipped by men (Rev. 19: 10; 22: 8, 9).

^^^

THE PRIESTHOOD - C TEACHES:

I. That the priest is the means of access between the sinner and God.

THE BIBLE TEACHES:

1. There is only one mediator, Christ (1 Tim. 2:5).

2. Christ said, "Come unto me. (Matt. 11: 28).

3. Paul said the only means of access is through Christ's blood (Heb. 9:14-22; 10:10-14).

4. Christ has the only unchangeable priesthood (Heb. 7:11, 12, 22-24).

5. There is only one earthly priesthood (Rev. 1: 5, 6; ALSO).

> **1Peter 2:5** Ye also, as lively stones, are built up a spiritual house, an holy priesthood, to offer up spiritual sacrifices, acceptable to God by Jesus Christ.

II. That priests should be called "father".

THE BIBLE TEACHES:

1. Christ said: "Call no man your father"

> **Matthew 23:9-10** And call no *man* your father upon the earth: for one is your Father, which is in heaven.
>
> 10 Neither be ye called masters: for one is your Master, *even* Christ.

III. That priests can absolve from sins, even though they are sinners themselves (Council of Trent).

THE BIBLE TEACHES:

1. Forgiveness of sins belongs to the Godhead (Mark 2: 6- 10; 1

John 1:9; 2:1)

^^

PURGATORY - C TEACHES:

I. That there is a place called Purgatory where the dead go to suffer punishment in order to be purified. (Introduced in the sixth century and made a church doctrine in the Council of Florence 1439)

THE BIBLE TEACHES:

1. The Scriptures teach against this

> **Hebrews 9:27** And as it is appointed unto men once to die, but after this the judgment:

2. Christ shows there is no second chance for the willful sinner here (Luke 16:19-31).

3. Bible knows nothing of indulgences either plenary or partial (Eph. 2: 3).

4. No such thing as purgatory is ever mentioned in the Scriptures.

NOTE: The Catholic Study Bible, the Oxford edition, does not list in its concordance - purgatory.

^^^

NAME - C TEACHES:

I. That the name to be worn is Catholic.

THE BIBLE TEACHES:

1. Adam and his wife wore the same name (Gen.5:2).

2. Adam is a figure of Christ (Rom. 5:14; 1 Cor.15:45).

3. Adam's wife, then, is a figure of Christ's wife, the church.

4 Adam and his wife wearing the same name pictured Christ and His wife wearing the same name.

5. Prophesied that a NEW name was to be given by the mouth of the Lord, when salvation went out from Jerusalem and the Gentiles saw His righteousness (Isa. 62: 1, 2).

6. The Prophecy fulfilled.

    (1.) Salvation went out from Jerusalem (Acts2:1-47).

    (2.) The Gentiles saw His righteousness (Acts10:1-48; 11:1).

(3.) The new name given (Acts 11:25, 20).

(4.) The name "Christian" means belonging to Christ.

7. We are married to Christ (Rom. 7:4).

8. King Agrippa knew Christ's followers wore the name Christian (Acts 26: 28)

9. Peter said we are to suffer in the name Christian

> **1Peter 4:16** Yet if *any man suffer* as a Christian, let him not be ashamed; but let him glorify God on this behalf.

10. No salvation promised in any other name (Acts 4: 12).

∧∧∧

SACRAMENTS - C TEACHES:

I. That there are seven sacraments:"five for the living and two for the dead."

NOTE: The word sacrament comes from Sacramentum", meaning an oath.

THE BIBLE TEACHES:

1. They are not spoken of as sacraments in the Bible.

2. There are only two ordinances of Christ, Baptism and the Lord's Supper.

∧∧∧

BAPTISM - C TEACHES:

I. The Catholic Church teaches that affusion, or sprinkling is sufficient for baptism.

THE BIBLE TEACHES:

1. Baptism is a birth (John 3:5).

2. Baptism is a washing (Acts 22:16).

3. Baptism is a burial (Rom. 6:4).

4. Baptism is a planting (Rom. 6:5).

5. Baptism is a resurrection (Col. 2:12).

6. There is ONE baptism

Eph. 4:5 One Lord, one faith, one baptism,

NOTE: Paul, who called baptism a burial planting, washing and a resurrection, said there is ONE baptism. He ought to know.

II. That an infant should be baptized.

THE BIBLE TEACHES:

1. Believers who repent are to be baptized (Mark 16:15, 16; ALSO).

> **Acts 2:38** Then Peter said unto them, Repent, and be baptized every one of you in the name of Jesus Christ for the remission of sins, and ye shall receive the gift of the Holy Ghost.

III. That the infant when baptized should be christened with the name of a saint and should have a godfather and a godmother.

THE BIBLE TEACHES:

1. Where is this doctrine or practice to be found anywhere?

∧∧

PENANCE - C TEACHES:

I. That the priests can forgive sins committed after baptism. (Lateran Council 1215.)

THE BIBLE TEACHES:

1. Forgiveness of sins belongs to the God-head. (Mark 2:6- 10; 1 John 1:9; ALSO)

> **1John 2:1** My little children, these things write I unto you, that ye sin not. And if any man sin, we have an advocate with the Father, Jesus Christ the righteous:

II. That sin can be forgiven by paying the priest to pray for the forgiveness of sins. Also those sinners can be prayed out of purgatory by paying the priest.

THE BIBLE TEACHES:

1. Redemption can not be purchased with gifts of silver or gold

(1 Peter 1:18).

∧∧

CONFIRMATION - C TEACHES:

I. That in confirmation we receive the Holy Spirit by the hands of the bishop.

THE BIBLE TEACHES:

1. Confirmation as such is not taught.

2. Christ the only one who can pray for the Holy Spirit to be sent

3. The Father only can confer the Holy Spirit.

> **John 14:15 -17** If ye love me, (Jesus) keep my commandments.
>
> 16 And I will pray the Father, and he shall give you another Comforter, that he may abide with you forever;
>
> 17 Even the Spirit of truth; whom the world cannot receive, because it seeth him not, neither knoweth him: but ye know him; for he dwelleth with you, and shall be in you.

∧∧

HOLY EUCHARIST - C TEACHES:

I. That the bread and fruit of the vine become the real body and blood of Christ at the consternation of the mass (Adopted by the church in the Council of Lateran 1215).

THE BIBLE TEACHES:

1. Christ was materially present "outside" of the bread and the fruit of the vine when He said, "This is my body," and "This is my blood" (Matt. 26: 26-28).

2. When Christ said He was a vine (John 15: 1) and a door (John 10: 9); He did not become a literal vine or door.

II. That the Lord's Supper is a sacrifice.

THE BIBLE TEACHES:

1. The Lord's Supper commemorates a "FINISHED" sacrifice (Luke 22: 19).

2. Repeating of Christ's sacrifice is forbidden (Heb. 6:6; 9:25, 26; 10:11, 12).

3. The Lord's Supper is not a sacrifice, but a remembrance (1 Cor. 11: 26).

III. That the fruit of the vine is only to be taken by the priests (Introduced in the Council of Constance 1414).

THE BIBLE TEACHES:

1. Both bread and fruit of the vine are to be given to all Christians (Matt. 26:27; Mark, 14: 23; 1 Cor. 11: 28).

IV. That the mass is the same sacrifice as that on the cross, only "un-bloody".

THE BIBLE TEACHES:

1. A bloody sacrifice is the only one known (Heb.10:10).

2. Only one sacrifice of Christ (Heb. 10: 12).

∧∧

EXTREME UNCTION - C TEACHES:

I. That this gives health and strength to the soul and sometimes to the body when one is at the point of death.

THE BIBLE TEACHES:

1. Where is the book, chapter and verse for such a practice?

∧∧

HOLY ORDERS - C TEACHES:

I. That holy orders are a sacrament by which the bishop, priests and officers of the church are ordained to office.

THE BIBLE TEACHES:

1. The Scriptures are silent on such a practice.

∧∧

MATRIMONY - C TEACHES:

I. That the marriage bond is a sacrament and offers grace.

THE BIBLE TEACHES:

1. The Scriptures are silent on such a practice, wherein the marriage is called a sacrament.

II. That marriage must be performed by a priest.

THE BIBLE TEACHES:

1. Where was the priest at the wedding Jesus attended? (John 2: 1-11).

III. That the marriage bond is never to be broken for any cause.

THE BIBLE TEACHES:

1. Scriptures give one reason for divorce-fornication (Matt. 5: 32).

^^

WORSHIP OF MARY - C TEACHES:

I. That Mary is immaculate, the Mother of God, spouse of the Holy Spirit, Proprietary of the world and the Gate of Heaven (Introduced as church doctrine by Pope Pius IX in 1854).

THE BIBLE TEACHES:

I. The Scriptures does not call her by such names.

2. If Mary's husband was the Holy Spirit, Joseph was illegally married to her.

3. The Scriptures teach that Mary was like other women, subject to their weaknesses. (Luke 2:22).

4. Jesus recognized Mary as only a human being. (John 2: 3, 4)

5. Mary realized Jesus was her Savior.

Luke 1:47 And my spirit hath rejoiced in God my Savior.

NOTE: The Mother of God would not need a savior.

6. The Scriptures accord worship to the baby and not to the mother.

7. Mary did not hold a superior position in the early church. She is only mentioned as attending a prayer meeting. (Acts 1; 14).

8. Mary commands men to follow Jesus, not her (John 2: 5).

> **Matt. 12:46-50**
>
> 46 While he yet talked to the people, behold, *his* mother and his brethren stood without, desiring to speak with him.
>
> 47 Then one said unto him, Behold, thy mother and thy brethren stand without desiring to speak with thee.
>
> 48 But he answered and said unto him that told him, Who is my mother? And who are my brethren?
>
> 49 And he stretched forth his hand toward his disciples, and said, Behold my mother and my brethren!
>
> 50 For whosoever shall do the will of my Father which is in heaven, the same is my brother, and sister, and mother.

^^

IMAGES - C TEACHES:

I. That it is not unscriptural to worship images. (Introduced in the Council of Trent)

THE BIBLE TEACHES;

1. The use of images forbidden (Ex. 20: 4; Isa.42; 8).

II. That they do not worship the image, but the one the image represents.

THE BIBLE TEACHES:

1. God said we, should have no graven images before Him (Ex. 20: 4).

NOTE: Catholicism ascribes to different images of the same personage different attributes, so they after all do make the image the object of worship.

∧∧

WORSHIP OF ANGELS - C TEACHES:

I. That one may pray to saints and angels. (Introduced during the sixth century)

THE BIBLE TEACHES:

1. Scriptures say the saints can not hear prayers (Ecl. 9:6).

2. Only one mediator between man and God (John 14: 6; 1 Tim. 2: 5).

3. Scriptures forbid angel worship (Col. 2: 18).

4. Angels are created servants and it would be idolatry to worship them

(Rev.22: 8, 9; ALSO)

> **Hebrews 1:5** For unto which of the angels said he at any time, Thou art my son, this day have I begotten thee? And again, I will be to him a Father, and he shall be to me a Son?
>
> 6 And again, when he bringeth in the first begotten into the world, he saith, And let all the angels of God worship him.
>
> 7 And of the angels he saith, Who maketh his angels spirits, and his ministers a flame of fire.
>
> 8 But unto the Son *he saith,* Thy throne, O God, *is* forever and ever: a scepter of righteousness *is* the scepter of thy kingdom.
>
> 9 Thou hast loved righteousness, and hated iniquity; therefore God, *even* thy God, hath anointed thee with the oil of gladness above thy fellows.
>
> 10 And, Thou, Lord, in the beginning hast laid the foundation of the earth; and the heavens are the works of thine hands:

11 They shall perish; but thou remainest; and they all shall wax old as doth a garment;

12 And as a vesture shalt thou fold them up, and they shall be changed: but thou art the same, and thy years shall not fail.

13 But to which of the angels said he at any time, Sit on my right hand, until I make thine enemies thy footstool?

14 Are they not all ministering spirits, sent forth to minister for them who shall be heirs of salvation?

∧∧

SUMMARY: Paul & Peter saw this apostate church coming.

I. Paul said:

1. He warned the elders of Ephesus (Acts 20: 29, 30).

> **Acts 20:30-31** Also of your own selves shall men arise, speaking perverse things, to draw away disciples after them.
>
> 31 Therefore watch, and remember, that by the space of three years I ceased not to warn every one night and day with tears.

2. He said grievous wolves were to arise from the eldership

(Acts 20: 30)

3. Grievous wolves did enter in from among ambitious elders and Peter admonished against such lording it over God's heritage

> **1Peter 5:3** Neither as being lords over *God's* heritage, but being examples to the flock.

4. There was a plurality of bishops or elders in each church, but no bishop or elder ever ruled over a plurality of churches until the apostasy came (Phil. 1:1; Acts 14: 23; ALSO).

> **Titus 1:5** For this cause left I thee in Crete, that thou shouldest set in order the things that are wanting, and ordain elders in every city, as I had appointed thee:

5. The apostasy came when bishops or elders were appointed over a district, archbishops over many districts, cardinals over all these and

finally a pope over all. Authority was usurped in writing creeds and binding them on the consciences of men.

6. Paul said, "The Spirit speaketh expressly, that in the latter times some shall depart from the faith, giving heed to seducing spirits and doctrines of devils. . . . forbidding to marry and commanding to abstain from meats"

> **1Timothy 4:1-3** Now the Spirit speaketh expressly, that in the latter times some shall depart from the faith, giving heed to seducing spirits, and doctrines of devils;
>
> 2 Speaking lies in hypocrisy; having their conscience seared with a hot iron;
>
> 3 Forbidding to marry, *and commanding* to abstain from meats, which God hath created to be received with thanksgiving of them which believe and know the truth.

NOTE: The Catholic Church, teaching the doctrines of devils, forbids her priests and sisters to marry and commands the church members to abstain from meats on certain days.

II. Peter said:

1. False teachers were to arise

> **2Peter 2:1** But there were false prophets also among the people, even as there shall be false teachers among you, who privily shall bring in damnable heresies, even denying the Lord that bought them, and bring upon themselves swift destruction.

III. Jude saw the same thing and realized it was a fulfillment of all the apostles had spoken concerning the falling away.

> **Jude 10-17** But these speak evil of those things which they know not: but what they know naturally, as brute beasts, in those things they corrupt themselves.

11 Woe unto them! For they have gone in the way of Cain, and ran greedily after the error of Balaam for reward, and perished in the gainsaying of Korah.

12 These are spots in your feasts of charity, when they feast with you, feeding themselves without fear: clouds *they are* without water, carried about of winds; trees whose fruit withereth, without fruit, twice dead, plucked up by the roots;

13 Raging waves of the sea, foaming out their own shame; wandering stars, to whom is reserved the blackness of darkness forever.

14 And Enoch also, the seventh from Adam, prophesied of these, saying, Behold, the Lord cometh with ten thousands of his saints,

15 To execute judgment upon all, and to convince all that are ungodly among them of all their ungodly deeds which they have ungodly committed, and of all their hard *speeches* which ungodly sinners have spoken against him.

16 These are murmurers, complainers, walking after their own lusts; and their mouth speaketh great swelling *words,* having men's persons in admiration because of advantage.

17 But, beloved, remember ye the words which were spoken before of the apostles of our Lord Jesus Christ;

2John 1:7-9 For many deceivers are entered into the world, who confess not that Jesus Christ is come in the flesh. This is a deceiver and an antichrist.

 8 Look to yourselves, that we lose not those things which we have wrought, but that we receive a full reward.

 9 Whosoever transgresseth, and abideth not in the doctrine of Christ, hath not God. He that abideth in the doctrine of Christ, he hath both the Father and the Son.

Matthew 13:24-55 Another parable put he forth unto them, saying, the kingdom of heaven is likened unto a man which sowed good seed in his field:

25 But while men slept, his enemy came and sowed tares among the wheat, and went his way.

26 But when the blade was sprung up, and brought forth fruit, then appeared the tares also.

27 So the servants of the householder came and said unto him, Sir, didst not thou sow good seed in thy field? From whence then hath it tares?

28 He said unto them, An enemy hath done this. The servants said unto him, Wilt thou then that we go and gather them up?

29 But he said, Nay; lest while ye gather up the tares, ye root up also the wheat with them.

30 Let both grow together until the harvest: and in the time of harvest I will say to the reapers, Gather ye together first the tares, and bind them in bundles to burn them: but gather the wheat into my barn.

31 Another parable put he forth unto them, saying, The kingdom of heaven is like to a grain of mustard seed, which a man took, and sowed in his field:

32 Which indeed is the least of all seeds: but when it is grown, it is the greatest among herbs, and becometh a tree, so that the birds of the air come and lodge in the branches thereof.

33 Another parable spake he unto them; The kingdom of heaven is like unto leaven, which a woman took, and hid in three measures of meal, till the whole was leavened.

34 All these things spake Jesus unto the multitude in parables; and without a parable spake he not unto them:

35 That it might be fulfilled which was spoken by the prophet, saying, I will open my mouth in parables; I will utter things which have been kept secret from the foundation of the world.

36 Then Jesus sent the multitude away, and went into the house: and his disciples came unto him, saying, Declare unto us the parable of the tares of the field.

37 He answered and said unto them, He that soweth the good seed is the Son of man;

38 The field is the world; the good seed are the children of the kingdom; but the tares are the children of the wicked *one*;

39 The enemy that sowed them is the devil; the harvest is the end of the world; and the reapers are the angels.

40 As therefore the tares are gathered and burned in the fire; so shall it be in the end of this world.

41 The Son of man shall send forth his angels, and they shall gather out of his kingdom all things that offend, and them which do iniquity;

42 And shall cast them into a furnace of fire: there shall be wailing and gnashing of teeth.

43 Then shall the righteous shine forth as the sun in the kingdom of their Father. Who hath ears to hear, let him hear.

44 Again, the kingdom of heaven is like unto treasure hid in a field; the which when a man hath found, he hideth, and for joy thereof goeth and selleth all that he hath, and buyeth that field.

45 Again, the kingdom of heaven is like unto a merchant man, seeking goodly pearls:

46 Who, when he had found one pearl of great price, went and sold all that he had, and bought it.

47 Again, the kingdom of heaven is like unto a net, that was cast into the sea, and gathered of every kind:

48 Which, when it was full, they drew to shore, and sat down, and gathered the good into vessels, but cast the bad away.

49 So shall it be at the end of the world: the angels shall come forth, and sever the wicked from among the just,

50 And shall cast them into the furnace of fire: there shall be wailing and gnashing of teeth.

51 Jesus saith unto them, Have ye understood all these things? They say unto him, Yea, Lord.

52 Then said he unto them, Therefore every scribe *which is* instructed unto the kingdom of heaven is like unto a man *that is* a householder, which bringeth forth out of his treasure *things* new and old.

53 And it came to pass, *that* when Jesus had finished these parables, he departed thence.

54 And when he was come into his own country, he taught them in their synagogue, insomuch that they were astonished, and said, Whence hath this *man* this wisdom, and *these* mighty works?

55 Is not this the carpenter's son? is not his mother called Mary? And his brethren, James, and Joses, and Simon, and Judas?

Popes of Dark Street

Serguis III - his mistress & her sister filled the papal chair with their paramours and bastard sons. (AD 904-963)

Boniface VII - murdered Pope John XIV

Benedict VIII- bought the office of Pope

John XIX - bought his office

Benedict IX - was made Pope at 12 years old by purchase from powerful families

He was called the worst of all Popes. He committed murders, adulteries, robbed pilgrims on the graves of martyrs and was driven out by the people.

Innocent III - claimed to be "Vicar of Christ," "Vicar of God," "Supreme Sovereign over the Church and the World" author of The Inquisition

Honorus III - gave papal sanction of torture of heretics (Christians not believing as they)

Gregory IX - gave papal sanction of torture of heretics

Innocent IV - gave papal sanction of torture of heretics

Nicolas V - authorized the King of Portugal to go to war on African peoples, to take their property and enslave people

Pipus II - father of many illegitimate children

Paul II - many concubines

Sixtus IV - Spanish Inquisition; made eight nephews Cardinals, some were just boys: lived lavish life style with his relatives.

Innocent VIII - 16 children by various married women.

Alexander VI - illegitimate children who were appointed to high church offices; murdered cardinals who stood in their way; other depravities.

To call these "men of God's calling" I can not. There are more but these are the worst of the worst.

Mormons

The "M" Church

Polygamy

Belief in many gods

A Christian priesthood

A completely anthropomorphic (human) God

These are some of the beliefs of this church.

The belief in "a second chance" was given to me by one of their members on my front porch, during the time I was in the process of assembling this work.

When I gave him back his "Book of Mormon" I slipped a card inside which looked like this:

~~~~~~~~~~

Read the Word of God (Bible). . .

Eternity is a long time to be wrong!

> **2John 1:9-11** Whosoever transgresseth, and abideth not in the doctrine of Christ, hath not God. He that abideth in the doctrine of Christ, he hath both the Father and the Son.

10. If there come any unto you, and bring not this doctrine, receive him not into *your* house, neither bid him Godspeed:

11. For he that biddeth him Godspeed is partaker of his evil deeds.

~~~~~~~~~~~

The fact that Sidney Rigdon talked about "The Book of Mormon," giving details only found in the book, years prior to its claim of authorship by Joseph Smith; and even before the two of them met, proves the conspiracy of a lie.

Mormonism

The Mormon Church was organized April 6,1830 at Fayette, N.Y. with six members by Joseph Smith, known as 'Peep-Stone' Joe, because following in the steps of his father as a roving water witch, he claimed to have miraculously discovered a 'peep-stone'. At the age of fourteen Smith began to have visions and revelations. According to his alleged statement three years later he had a vision one night in which the angel Moroni appeared unto him and revealed the hiding place of certain plates of gold on which were inscribed the Gospel. With the aid of Harris, Cowdery, and Whitmer, Smith is supposed to have translated this writing into what is now the Book of the Mormon. In 1831 Smith and a small company of converts moved to Kirkland, Ohio, but because of a scandal which occurred there they moved to Missouri. Trouble breaking out there, Smith and about fifteen thousand followers went to Nauvoo, Ill. It was here that the doctrine of polygamy was introduced, although Mormons had been accused before this of unholy relationships with numerous women.

Internal trouble arose at Nauvoo, and public opinion ran high against the Mormons. Finally, Smith & his brother, Hyrum, were arrested on a charge of treason and lodged in the jail at Carthage. Here a mob broke into the jail and shot the two brothers. After Smith's death the Mormons split into several divisions. One under the leadership of J.J. Sprang went to Wisconsin, but died out upon the death of its leader; another group formed the Reorganized Church of Jesus Christ of Latter Day Saints. But the main body, under the leadership of Brigham Young, immigrated in 1848 to Utah. This, even today, is by far the largest body of Mormons and has its headquarters in Salt Lake City.

~~~~~~

A SECOND CHANCE- M TEACHES

I. A second chance

The Bible teaches:

> **Heb. 9:27** And as it is appointed unto men once to die, but after this the judgment:

~~~~~~

GOD-M TEACHES

I. There are many gods: (Key of Theology, page 52)

The Bible teaches:

1. There is only one God with three in the Godhead

> **John 16:7-10** Nevertheless I tell you the truth; It is expedient for you that I go away: for if I go not away, the Comforter will not come unto you; but if I depart,   I will send him unto you.
>
> 8 And when he is come, he will reprove the world of sin, and of righteousness, and of judgment:
>
> 9 Of sin, because they believe not on me;
>
> 10 Of righteousness, because I go to my Father, and ye see me no more; (Also: Gen. 1:26; Ex.20:1-3; Matt.28:19; John 1:1-3; John14:25, 26)

II. These Gods have bodies of bones &flesh. (D. & C., sec. 130:22)

The Bible teaches:

1. God is an omnipresent Being. (Psa. 139:7-11; Acts 17:28;

1 Cor. 3:16)

2. God is an omniscient Being. (Job 34:21; Prov. 15:3; John 2:24, 25)

3. God is an omnipotent Being. (Gen 1:1; Psa. 8:3; John 1:1-3)

Note: If God had flesh & bones, He couldn't be any of these three.

4. God is a spirit.

> **John 4:24** God *is* a Spirit: and they that worship him must worship *him* in spirit and in truth. (Jesus)(Also: Luke 24:39; 1 Cor. 15:50)

III. That the gods have sex and marry and bear children and their children come to this world as human beings to get bodies. (Compendium (B) 287, Last sermon 1844; Key of Theology, page 41, 52; The Seer, Vol. 1, page 37)

The Bible teaches:

1. God's only marriage relationship is with Israel. (Jer. 3:14)

2. Christ's only marriage relationship is with Christians. (Eph. 5:23-33)

3. Christ is the husband and head of the Church. (John 3:29; Col. 1:18)

4. There is no marriage relationship after death.

> **Mark 12:25** For when they shall rise from the dead, they neither marry, nor are given in marriage; but are as the angels which are in heaven. (Jesus)

IV. That Adam is a God. (Pearl of Great Price, page 60)

The Bible teaches: Adam was a man created by God.

> **Gen 1:27** So God created man in his *own* image, in the image of God created he him; male and female created he them. (Also: Gen 2:18, 20-25; 3:8-11, 19; Ex. 20: 1-3)

V. That God is an exalted man who was once as we are and that we are to become like him.

(Journal of Discourses, Vol 6, page 3, & page 5, sermons by Joseph Smith)

The Bible teaches:

1. Man is a created being. (Gen 2:7)

2. Christ from His fleshly side only was like us. (Isa. 7:14; Matt. 1:20-23)

3. No man has ascended into heaven but Christ, proving that Adam or none before Christ ever went to heaven and that none could have become Gods.

> **John 3:13** And no man hath ascended up to heaven, but he that came down from heaven, *even* the Son of man which is in heaven.(Jesus)

~~~~~~

JESUS-M TEACHES

I. Christ was the son of Adam. (Journal of Discourses, Vol1, page 50, sermon by Brigham Young)

The Bible teaches:

1. Christ was born of the Holy Spirit.

> **Isaiah 7:14** Therefore the Lord himself shall give you a sign; Behold, a virgin shall conceive, and bear a son, and shall call his name Immanuel. (Also: Matt. 1: 18-23

II. That Jesus was a polygamist. (The Seer, Vol. 1, page 158-159)

The Bible teaches:

1. Christ is the husband of the Church.

> **Romans 7:4** Wherefore, my brethren, ye also are become dead to the law by the body of Christ; that ye should be married to another, *even* to him who is raised from the dead, that we should bring forth fruit unto God. (Also: John 3:29; Eph. 5:23-33)

~~~~~~

THE HOLY SPIRIT - M TEACHES

I. That the Holy Spirit is ethereal substance diffused through space, the purest and most refined of substances.

The Bible teaches:

1. The Holy Spirit is a personality.

> **Matthew 28:19** Go ye therefore, and teach all nations, baptizing them in the name of the Father, and of the Son, and of the Holy Ghost: (also: John 14: 15-17; John 16: 13,14; Acts 5:3,4; 8:29; 10:19, 20; 1 John 5:7)

II. That there is only one mode by which the Holy Spirit is conferred and that is by laying on of hands.

The Bible teaches:

1. The Holy Spirit is given in three degrees.

1. Baptismal. (Acts 2:1-4; 10:44-47; 11:15)

2. By laying on of an apostle's hands (Acts 8:12-17; 19:6; 1 Tim. 4:14; 2 Tim. 4:6)

NOTE: None but an apostle could confer the Holy Spirit by laying on of hands and the apostles have no successors

3. The general gift of the Holy Spirit after baptism as a Comforter or counselor.

John 14:15-17 (Jesus) If ye love me, keep my commandments.

16 And I will pray the Father, and he shall give you another Comforter, that he may abide with you forever;

17 Even the Spirit of truth; whom the world cannot receive, because it seeth him not, neither knoweth him: but ye know him; for he dwelleth with you, and shall be in you. (Also: Acts 2:39)

~~~~~~

THE BIBLE - M TEACHES

I. That the Bible is not all the Word of God. (D. and C Sec. 84: 57; 42:17)

(Book of Mormon, II Nephi 12:53-64)

II. That the Book of Mormon and the Doctrine and Covenants are on par with the Bible. (Catechism, Chap. III, Questions 1 & 2)

III. That the Bible has scarcely a verse that is not polluted. (Divine Authenticity of the Book of Mormon, pages 204, 205, 218, Orson Pratt)

The Bible teaches:

Isaiah 8:20 To the law and to the testimony: if they speak not according to this word, *it is* because *there is* no light in them.

Rev. 22:18-19 For I testify unto every man that heareth the words of the prophecy of this book, if any man shall add unto these things, God shall add unto him the plagues that are written in this book:

19 And if any man shall take away from the words of the book of this prophecy, God shall take away his part out of the book of life, and out of the holy city, and *from* the things which are written in this book.

^^

Concerning the plates found by Joseph Smith.

The Egyptian hieroglyphics in 1833 had not been fully deciphered, and there was no way of proving Smith's work. However, in 1861 Smith's translation was shown to a scholar named Theodule Deveria of Paris, who declared the work was "entirely incorrect". So also attest eight other scholars in Egyptian lore. (Snowden, Ibid., pp. 76-79)

> **1Th. 5:21** Prove all things; hold fast that which is good.

> **1Cor. 14:33** For God is not *the author* of confusion, but of peace, as in all churches of the saints.

Jehovah Witnesses

The "J W" Church

This is the church that has its members show up at your door step offering to show you their version of the bible.

Do not be persuaded by these well meaning people. The "New World Translation" has been re- written towards their beliefs. It is a perverted Word of God.

I have placed a copy of the 23rd psalm at the end of this section. There are two versions, the one you knew as a child and the one according to the N. W. Translation.

You decide.

2Thess. 2:11 And for this cause God shall send them strong delusion, that they should believe a lie:

Jehovah's Witness

The organizer of this movement was Charles Taze Russell (1854-1916). He embraced Adventism early in life, but at the age of 20 abandoned it primarily due to his opinion that the date fixed by Wm. Miller was erroneous. He insisted that the date of the Second Advent was 1874, the same year he began to preach. It seemed not to matter to him that Jesus had said that neither the Son, nor the angels knew, but "the Father only". (Mark 13:32).

"Pastor" Russell formally organized his followers in Pittsburgh, with himself as president. Headquarters were moved to Brooklyn, New York, in 1909. It is reported that 13,000,000 of Russell's Studies in the Scriptures (Volumes1-6) have been circulated. These laid the foundation for the new sect known before 1931 as Millennial Dawnests, International Bible Students, and Russellites.

In his six volumes (he prophesied he would write seven, but death overtook him before the task was finished.) he maintained that the plan of God was unfolded and made known through him "as never before," and added that "the opening of the books of divine revelation will soon be completed" (Vol. 2 ,pg 189). In addition to this claim of "divine revelation," Russell maintained that probably never before had anyone (This would include the apostles!) "understood any part" of the book of Revelation (1, pg. 27)

It is the old story of an ambitious man claiming that the Bible truths are hidden "from all except the consecrated" (Finished Mystery, pg. 65), and saying, "Lo! Here is my writing, the long awaited true explanation." Russell's first book was published in 1866 which he entitled <u>Millennial Dawn</u>. The name was changed to <u>Studies in the Scriptures</u> in 1916.

After "Pastor" Russell's death in 1916, his adherents were slowly culled out and pushed out of the newer organization now headed by Judge

Rutherford. Russell's old Watchtower Society passed into oblivion by federal court order in 1918. Finally, with all of Russell partisans out of the way, it was evident to all of Russell's adherents that a new name would have to be selected. This new name was given at a convention held in Columbus, Ohio, October, 1931 (Theocracy, pg. 34). The new name, Jehovah's Witnesses, identified the new sect headed by Rutherford.

In an effort to cover up the newness of the name, it was contended that Jehovah had witnesses from the time of Abel, and that Isaiah. 62:2 prophesied the giving of the new name in 1931. Each issue of the Watchtower magazine carries these words on the cover. "You are my witnesses, says Jehovah - Isa.43:12"

Without the Watchtower hierarchy, the slaves would pass into oblivion as sheep without a shepherd. . . And this is precisely what the Watchtower said would happen to a man who lays Russell's books down and reads the Bible only! "Within two years, he goes into darkness!" (Sept 10, 1910, pg. 298)

Today, the Watchtower Bible and Tract Society with main headquarters in Brooklyn, N.Y., prints over 100 million copies of their material in some 80 languages each year

~~~~~~

J.W. teaches:

I. That one can not have true light without the help of "Studies in the Scriptures".

(Watch Tower, Sept. 15, 1910, page 298)

The Bible teaches:

1. God's Word is a lamp & a light and is sufficient to perfect the man of God.

2Timothy 3:16 All Scripture *is* given by inspiration of God, and *is* profitable for doctrine, for reproof, for correction, for instruction in righteousness:

That the man of God may be perfect, thoroughly furnished unto all good works. (Also: Psalm 119:105)

~~~~~~

GOD- JW TEACHES

I. There is only one person in the God-head. (Vol. 5, page 166)

The Bible teaches:

1. Baptism is into the name of three personalities.

> **Matthew 28:19** Go ye therefore, and teach all nations, baptizing them in the name of the Father, and of the Son, and of the Holy Ghost:

2. Christ taught three personalities in the God-head.

> **John 14:15-16** If ye love me, keep my commandments.
>
> 16. And I will pray the Father, and he shall give you another comforter, that he may abide with you forever;

> **John 14:26** But the Comforter, *which is* the Holy Ghost, whom the Father will send in my name, he shall teach you all things, and bring all 0things to your remembrance, whatsoever I have said unto you (Also: John 15:26)

~~~~~~

CHRIST - JW TEACHES

I. That Christ was a 'created angel' before He came to this earth. (Vol. 5, page 84)

The Bible teaches:

1. Christ was more than an angel.

> **Heb 1:1-8** God who at sundry times and in divers (various) manners spake in time past unto the fathers by the prophets,
>
> 2 Hath in these last days spoken unto us by *his* Son, whom he hath appointed heir of all things, by whom also he made the worlds;

3 Who being the brightness of *his* glory, and the express image of his person, and upholding all things by the word of his power, when he had by himself purged our sins, sat down on the right hand of the Majesty on high;

4 Being made so much better than the angels, as he hath by Inheritance obtained a more excellent name than they.

5 For unto which of the angels said he at any time, Thou art my son, this day have I begotten thee? And again, I will be to him a Father, and he shall be to me a Son?

6 And again, when he bringeth in the first begotten into the world, he saith, And let all the angels of God worship him.

7 And of the angels he saith, Who maketh his angels spirits, and his ministers a flame of fire.

8 But unto the Son *he saith,* Thy throne, O God, *is* forever and ever: a scepter of righteousness *is* the scepter of thy kingdom.

2. Christ was not created - He was eternal. John 1:1-3; 8:58; Rev. 1:8; 21:6; 22:13)

II. That Christ was not a combination of two natures - human & divine.

(Vol. 1, page 179)

The Bible teaches:

1. Prophesied that God would tabernacle in the flesh. (Isa 7:14;

Matt. 1:23)

2. Christ was begotten of the Holy Spirit and born of Mary, making two natures, human & divine.

Mat 1:18-20 Now the birth of Jesus Christ was on this wise: When as his mother Mary was espoused to Joseph, before they came together, she was found with child of the Holy Ghost.

19 Then Joseph her husband, being a just *man,* and not willing to make her a public example, was minded to put her away secretly.

20 But while he thought on these things, behold, the angel of the Lord appeared unto him in a dream, saying, Joseph, thou son of David, fear not to take unto thee Mary thy wife; for that which is conceived in her is of the Holy Ghost.

3. Christ was made in the likeness of man. (Phil. 2:6, 7; Heb. 2:16)

4. Christ was human and divine

1Timothy 3:16 And without controversy great is the mystery of godliness: God was manifest in the flesh, justified in the Spirit, seen of angels, preached unto the Gentiles, believed on in the world, received up into glory.(Also: John 1:1,2, 14; 16:28)

5. Peter confessed Him as the Son of God. (Matt. 16:16)

6. He who doesn't confess that Christ came in the flesh is a deceiver and not of God.

1John 4:3 And every spirit that confesseth not that Jesus Christ is come in the flesh is not of God: and this is that *spirit* of antichrist, whereof ye have heard that it should come; and even now already is it in the world.

2John 1:7 For many deceivers are entered into the world, who confess not that Jesus Christ is come in the flesh. This is a deceiver and an antichrist.

III. That Christ did not atone for the sins of man. (Vol. 5, page 95)

The Bible teaches:

1. Christ takes away sins.

John 1:29 The next day John seeth Jesus coming unto him, and saith, Behold the Lamb of God, which taketh away the sin of the world.(Also: Matt. 10:28; Rom. 5:11; Heb. 10: 3-14)

IV. That Christ's body was not raised from the dead. (Vol. 2, pages 125-130)

V. That Christ is dead forever. (Vol. 5, page 443)

The Bible teaches:

1. Jesus said He would raise His body. (John 2:19-22)

2. Jesus showed Thomas His raised body. (John 20: 24-28)

3. Prophesied that Christ would be resurrected. (Psalms 16:10)

4. Peter said Christ was raised from the dead. (Acts 2:30, 31)

5. Christ showed Himself alive by many infallible proofs. (Acts 1:1-3)

6. Christ was seen alive by many brethren.

> **1Co 15:1-8** Moreover, brethren, I declare unto you the gospel which I preached unto you, which also ye have received, and wherein ye stand;
>
> 2 By which also ye are saved, if ye keep in memory what I preached unto you, unless ye have believed in vain.
>
> 3 For I delivered unto you first of all that which I also received, how that Christ died for our sins according to the Scriptures;
>
> 4 And that he was buried, and that he rose again the third day according to the Scriptures:
>
> 5 And that he was seen of Cephas, then of the twelve:
>
> 6 After that, he was seen of above five hundred brethren at once; of whom the greater part remain unto this present, but some are fallen asleep.
>
> 7 After that, he was seen of James; then of all the apostles.
>
> 8 And last of all he was seen of me also, as of one born out of due time.

VI. That Jesus was not divine until after His resurrection. (Vol. 1, page 179)

The Bible teaches:

1. Christ was always divine.

John 17:5 And now, O Father, glorify thou me with thine own self with the glory which I had with thee before the world was. (Jesus)(Also: John 1:1-3)

2. Christ was equal with God. (Phil. 2:6)

3. Christ and God are one. (John 14:11; 17:21)

VII. That Christ was no longer the same person after the resurrection.

The Bible teaches:

1. He is the same person after resurrection.

> **Ephesians 4:10** He that descended is the same also that ascended up far above all heavens, that he might fill all things. (Also: Acts 1:11; Hebrews 10:12)

VIII. That Christ is not a mediator. (Watch Tower, Sept 15, 1909, page 283)

The Bible teaches:

1. Jesus Christ is our mediator.

> **1Timothy 2:5** For *there is* one God, and one mediator between God and men, the man Christ Jesus;

~~~~~~

THE HOLY SPIRIT - JW TEACHES

I. That the Holy Spirit is only the influence or power exercised by the one God.

(Vol 5, page 165)

The Bible teaches:

1. The Holy Spirit is part of the God-head. (Matt 3:16, 17; Matt. 28:19)

2. The Holy Spirit is called God.

Act 5:3-4 But Peter said, Ananias, why hath Satan filled thine heart to lie to the Holy Ghost, and to keep back *part* of the price of the land?

4 While it remained, was it not thine own? and after it was sold, was it not in thine own power? why hast thou conceived this thing in thine heart? thou hast not lied unto men, but unto God.

~~~~~~

THE KINGDOM - JW TEACHES

I. That the kingdom is not yet established. (Vol. 1, page 172)

II. That the kingdom is not to be established until the millennium. (Vol. 1, page 83)

The Bible teaches:

1. John & Jesus preached the kingdom at hand in their day. (Matt.3:2; 4:17)

2. Jesus said some in His generation would not taste death until the kingdom should come. (Matt. 16:28; Mark 9:1)

3. We today are translated in the kingdom of God's dear Son.

> **Col 1:13** Who hath delivered us from the power of darkness, and hath translated *us* into the kingdom of his dear Son:

NOTE: How could we be translated into a kingdom if it didn't already exist?

~~~~~~

SIN - JW TEACHES

I. That each does not die for his own sin, but for Adam's sin. (Vol. 1, page 109)

The Bible teaches:

1. We die for our own sin.

> **Romans 5:12** Wherefore, as by one man sin entered into the world, and death by sin; and so death passed upon all men, for that all have sinned:
>
> **Romans 3:23** For all have sinned, and come short of the glory of God;

HELL - JW TEACHES

I. That there is no eternal punishment. (Vol. 1, page 159)

The Bible teaches:

1. There is an eternal punishment.

> **Matthew 25:46** And these shall go away into everlasting punishment: but the righteous into life eternal. (Jesus)
>
> (Also: Dan 12:2; John5:28, 29; Rev. 20:10)

~~~~~~

TIME SETTING - JW TEACHES

I. That the apostles and Christ have been living on the earth since 1874 as invisible spirits in bodily form. (Vol 2, pages 170, 171, 234)

The Bible teaches:

1. Christ says no man, angel or even He knows the day or the hour.

(Mark 13:32)

2. At Christ's return the dead Christians are to be raised and the living

Christians are to be translated.

> **1Thessalonians 4:13-17** But I would not have you to be ignorant, brethren, concerning them which are asleep, that ye sorrow not, even as others which have no hope.
>
> 14 For if we believe that Jesus died and rose again, even so them also which sleep in Jesus will God bring with him.
>
> 15 For this we say unto you by the word of the Lord, that we which are alive *and* remain unto the coming of the Lord shall not prevent them which are asleep.
>
> 16 For the Lord himself shall descend from heaven with a shout, with the voice of the archangel, and with the trump of God: and the dead in Christ shall rise first:
>
> 17 Then we which are alive *and* remain shall be caught up together with them in the clouds to meet the Lord in the air: and so shall we ever be with the Lord.

NOTE: Mr. Russell and his "little flock" must have been overlooked.

II. That all worldly kingdoms will end in 1914 and the Church of Christ will be set up with Christ at the head. (Vol. 2, page 170

III. That the harvest of the Gospel age was to end in 1914.

"Remember that the forty years of Jewish harvest ended Oct., A.D. 69, and was followed by the complete overthrow of that nation; and that likewise the forty years of the gospel age harvest will end Oct., 1914, and that likewise the overthrow of Christendom, so called, must be to immediately follow." (Vol. 2, page 245).

The Bible teaches:

1. 1914 is history and this did not come to pass.

2. No man knows the day or the hour.

> **Mark 13:32** But of that day and *that* hour knoweth no man, no, not the angels which are in heaven, neither the Son, but the Father. (Jesus)

Psalm 23   (JW verses KJV)

Psalm 23 according to the King James Version of the Word of God

1 A Psalm of David. The LORD *is* my shepherd; I shall not want.

2 He maketh me to lie down in green pastures: he leadeth me beside the still waters.

3 He restoreth my soul: he leadeth me in the paths of righteousness for his name's sake.

4 Yea, though I walk through the valley of the shadow of death, I will fear no evil: for thou *art* with me; thy rod and thy staff they comfort me.

5 Thou preparest a table before me in the presence of mine enemies: thou anointest my head with oil; my cup runneth over.

6 Surely goodness and mercy shall follow me all the days of my life: and I will dwell in the house of the LORD forever.

~~~~~~

Psalm 23 according to New World Translation (JW)

1 A melody of David. Jehovah *is* my shepherd; I shall lack nothing.

2 In grassy pastures he makes me lie down: By well-watered resting places he conducts me.

3 My soul he refreshes: He leads me in the tracks of righteousness for his name's sake.

4 Even though I walk in the valley of deep shadow, I fear nothing bad, for you *are* with me; Your rod and your staff are the things that comfort me.

5 You arrange before me a table in front of those showing hostility to me. With oil you have greased my head; my cup is well filled.

6 Surely goodness and loving kindness themselves will pursue me all the days of my life: and I will dwell in the house of Jehovah to the length of days.

Christian Science

The "C S" Church

This church is neither Christian nor science.

From a book I received while recovering from a stroke, I read that if I went back to the place where the stroke occurred, I could wipe it out of my memory and cure myself. I believe I'll trust God for that.

I also learned that it is possible by shouting at the dead to bring them back to life.

When I sent this book back to the friend who sent it, I enclosed a note in which said that in order for this to work, one really needed faith, to which the reply from her was, "You don't need faith. Just do it!"

In all things, I'll put my trust in whom I have believed

> **2Peter 2:1** But there were false prophets also among the people, even as there shall be false teachers among you, who will secretly bring in damnable heresies, even denying the Lord that bought them, and bring upon themselves swift destruction.

Christian Science

Early in the nineteenth Century there appeared in Portland, Me., a mental healer, Dr. Quimby by name who experimented in healing by mesmerism and hypnotism. From 1862 to 1865 he had a now noted patient - Mrs. Eddy - who in early womanhood attracted some attention as a mesmeric subject. Claiming to be healed by Dr. Quimby she became a student and advocate of his teachings. Dr. Quimby died in 1865 and in 1866 Mrs. Eddy had a timely revelation in which she claimed to have discovered the teachings of Christian Science. These teachings she incorporated into a book called Science and Health, and after copywriting it, sold it through many editions at a handsome revenue. A close comparison of Mrs. Eddy's Science and Health and Dr. Quimby's Science of Man will startle any reader by their similitude.

The first edition of the book appeared in 1875 and has gone through many changes, transpositions, and with each change a rich harvest has been reaped from the sale of new editions. In 1876 Mrs. Eddy organized the first Christian Science Association with six pupils. In 1879 she organized the first Science Church in Boston with twenty six members and herself as pastor. This became the mother church. The membership of Christian Science Churches runs in the ratio of about three women to every man.

Mrs. Eddy was married three times, once divorced, and in many ways her career was a checkered one. She reaped handsomely from the revenue obtained from healings, lessons on healing, sale of Christian Science spoons, books and other remunerative methods. She died reported to be worth over three million dollars.

C.S. Teaches:

I. That thru their books they have found a way to salvation.

The Bible teaches:

1. There is only one way.

> **John 14:6** Jesus saith unto him, I am the way, the truth, and the life: no man cometh unto the Father, but by me.
>
> **1Timothy 6:20** O Timothy, keep that which is committed to thy trust, avoiding profane *and* vain babblings, and oppositions of science falsely so called:
>
> **2John 1:7** For many deceivers are entered into the world, who confess not that Jesus Christ is come in the flesh. This is a deceiver and an antichrist.
>
> **2Timothy 3:13** But evil men and seducers shall wax worse and worse, deceiving, and being deceived.

~~~~~~

THE BIBLE - CS TEACHES

I. That the Bible is impure.

A moral and material sense stole into the divine record, with its own hue darkening to some extent the inspired pages. (S. & H 139: 20-22)

The Bible teaches:

> **Proverbs 30:5** Every word of God *is* pure: he *is* a shield unto them that put their trust in him. (Also: Rom. 3:4; 2 Tim. 3:16; 2 Peter 1:2)

II. That some of the pages of the Bible are lies.

Regarding Gen. 2:7 - Is it the truth, or is it a lie concerning man and God? It must be a lie. (S. & H 524: 25-27)

The Bible teaches:

> **Isaiah 8:20** To the law and to the testimony: if they speak not according to this word, *it is* because *there is* no light in them. (Also: Rom. 3:4)

III. That the Bible does not contain all revelation.

God had been graciously preparing me during many years for the reception of this final revelation. (S. &H. 107:3-5

The Bible teaches:

> **Proverbs 30:6** Add thou not unto his words, lest he reprove thee, and thou be found a liar. (Also: Rev. 22:18-19)

~~~~~~

GOD - CS TEACHES

I. That God is incorporeal, divine, supreme, infinite mind, soul, spirit, principal, truth love. (S. & H. 465:8-10)

I knew the principal of all harmonious mind-action to be God. (S. & H. 109:16, 17)

The Bible teaches:

1. God is a personality.

> **Hebrews 1:3** Who being the brightness of *his* glory, and the express image of his person, and upholding all things by the word of his power, when he had by himself purge our sins, sat down on the right hand of the Majesty on high;
>
> (Also: Gen. 1: 1-31)

~~~~~~

JESUS CHRIST - CS TEACHES

I. That Christ is not God.

Jesus Christ is not God, as Jesus Himself declared, but is the Son of God. This declaration of Jesus, understood, conflicts not at all with another of His sayings: "I and my Father are one, that is, one in quality, not in quantity. As a drop of water is one with the ocean, a ray of light one with the sun, even so God and man, Father and Son, are one in being. (S. & H. 36: 12-8.)

The Bible teaches:

1. Christ is called God.

> **Hebrews 1:8** But unto the Son *he saith,* Thy throne, O God, *is* forever and ever: a scepter of righteousness *is* the scepter of thy kingdom. (Isa. 9:6; John 20:28; Phil. 2:5)

II. That Jesus was not incarnated in the flesh.

Those instructed in Christian Science have reached the glorious perception that God isn't the only author of man. The Virgin Mother conceived this idea of God, and gave to this ideal the name of Jesus. (S. &H. 29:14-18)

Jesus was the offspring of Mary's self-conscious communion with God. (S. &H 29:32; 30:1)

The Bible teaches:

1. Jesus was incarnated in the flesh.

> **John 1:14** And the Word was made flesh, and dwelt among us, (and we beheld his glory, the glory as of the only begotten of the Father,) full of grace and truth. (Also: Luke 1: 30, 31, 34, and 35)

III. That every spiritual idea is a child.

When a new scriptural idea is born to earth the prophetic scripture of Isaiah is renewably fulfilled, "unto us a child is born". (S. &H. 109:24-27)

The Bible teaches:

1. Jesus came to fulfill (Isa. 9:6) and he had flesh & bones.

> **Luke 24:39** Behold my hands and my feet, that it is I myself: handle me, and see; for a spirit hath not flesh and bones, as ye see me have. (Jesus)

IV. That Christ is not a man, but an ideal truth. (475:10-17; 332:11, 12)

The Bible teaches:

1. That Jesus & Christ are the same person and had a fleshly body. (John 20:31; Romans 5:8, 1 Corinthians 5:3; 1 Peter 1:19; Eph. 2: 13-16)

2. That a man is a liar who denies Jesus & Christ is the same.

> **1John 2:22** Who is a liar but he that denieth that Jesus is the Christ? He is antichrist, that denieth the Father and the Son.

3. That he is a **deceiver** who does not confess that Jesus Christ is come in the flesh. (2 John 7)

V. That Christ didn't actually die. (46:2, 3; 44:28, 29; 45:11)

The Bible teaches:

1. He actually died.

> **John 19:33** But when they came to Jesus, and saw that he was dead already, they broke not his legs: (Also: Romans 5:8; 14:9; 15:3)

VI. That the blood of Christ does not cleanse the sinner of sin. (25:6-9)

> NOTE: Since Jesus & Christ are the same person, (see 4 above) , then here is an admittance that He came in the flesh and that blood coursed through His veins, which contradicts the statement that Christ did not come in the flesh.

The Bible teaches:

1. We are cleansed by Christ's blood.

> **1John 1:7** But if we walk in the light, as he is in the light, we have fellowship one with another, and the blood of Jesus Christ his Son cleanseth us from all sin. (Also: Rom. 5:9; Col. 1:20; Heb. 10:4-12)

VII. That Christ didn't physically rise from the dead. (313:26-30)

The Bible teaches:

1. Jesus said He physically rose from the dead.

> **John 20:26-29** And after eight days again his disciples were within, and Thomas with them: *then* came Jesus, the doors being shut, and stood in the midst, and said, Peace, *be* unto you.
>
> 27Then saith he to Thomas, Reach hither thy finger, and behold my hands; and reach hither thy hand, and thrust *it* into my side: and be not faithless, but believing.
>
> 28And Thomas answered and said unto him, My Lord and my God.
>
> 29Jesus saith unto him, Thomas, because thou hast seen me, thou hast believed: blessed *are* they that have not seen, and *yet* have believed. (Also: Luke 24:39-43)

VIII. That Jesus didn't ascend in His physical body. (334:14-17)

The Bible teaches:

1. Jesus did indeed ascend into heaven.

> **Luke 24:50-51** And he led them out as far as to Bethany, and he lifted up his hands, and blessed them.
>
> 51 And it came to pass, while he blessed them, he was parted from them, and carried up into heaven. (Also: Acts 7:55; 9:5; Heb. 4:14)

IX. That Jesus will not return in the bodily form. (Retrospection and Introspection 70:20-22)

The Bible teaches:

1. He will return in the same manner He left.

> **Acts 1:11** Which also said, Ye men of Galilee, why stand ye gazing up into heaven? this same Jesus, which is taken up from you into heaven, shall so come in like manner as ye have seen him go into heaven.

~~~~~~

THE TRINITY - CS TEACHES

I. That there are not three persons in the one God-head. (256:9-11; 515:17-19)

The Bible teaches:

1. God Said, "let **US** make man in **OUR** own image. (Gen 1:26)

2. Christ commanded baptism into three persons of the God-head. (Matt. 28:19)

3. Christ came in the express image of God's person. (Heb 1:3)

God, then, is a person, showing that the three in the God-head are persons.

~~~~~~

THE DEVIL - CS TEACHES

I. That the devil is a lie and an error. (584:17-19; 187:10-12)

The Bible:

1. There is a devil.

> **Luke 22:31** And the Lord said, Simon, Simon, behold, Satan hath desired *to have* you, that he may sift *you* as wheat: (Also: Rev. 12:9, 12; Matt. 4:11)

2. Christ said the devil is a liar.

> **John 8:44** Ye are of *your* father the devil, and the lusts of your father ye will do. He was a murderer from the beginning, and abode not in the truth, because there is no truth in him. When he speaketh a lie, he speaketh of his own: for he is a liar, and the father of it.

~~~~~~

SIN - CS TEACHES

I That it is impossible for man to fall into sin (258:27-30; 428:22, 23)

II. That sin is an illusion. (283:8-11)

The Bible teaches:

1. There is no man that does not sin. (1 Kings 8:46)

2. Christ said men sin. (Luke 7:47)

3. The Holy Spirit is to reprove the world of sin (John 16:8)

4. Paul said that all have sinned & come short of the glory of God. (Romans 3:23)

5. The Apostle John says:

1John 1:8-9 If we say that we have no sin, we deceive ourselves, and the truth is not in us.

9 If we confess our sins, he is faithful and just to forgive us *our* sins, and to cleanse us from all unrighteousness.

III. That to get rid of sin is to divest sin of any supposed reality. (339:28-30

The Bible teaches:

Col 2:13 And you, being dead in your sins and the uncircumcision of your flesh, hath he quickened together with him, having forgiven you all trespasses ;(Also: Matt. 9:6; Eph. 1:7)

IV. That man can not sin. (475:28; 481:28)

The Bible teaches:

Romans 3:23 For all have sinned, and come short of the glory of God. (Also: 1 Kings 8:46)

V. That there is no such thing as sickness, disease or pain. (285:8, 9, 11; 393:29; 421:18)

The Bible teaches:

Matthew 4:24 And his fame went throughout all Syria: and they brought unto him all sick people that were taken with divers diseases and torments, and those which were possessed with devils, and those which were lunatic, and those that had the palsy; and he healed them. (Also: Mark 6:5; John 4:46)

VI. That growing old is an illusion. (245:30-31)

The Bible teaches:

> **Proverbs 16:31** The hoary[7872] head *is* a crown of glory, *if* it be found in the way of righteousness.

H7872 ---   Strong's Hebrew & Greek Dictionary

שׂיבה

śe^yba^h

say-baw'

Feminine of H7869; **old** *age:* - (be) **gray** (grey, hoar, -y) **hairs**

VII. That there is no death. (75:13-15; 584:9)

The Bible teaches:

1. Man has died from the beginning. (Gen. 5:1-5)

2. Jesus said plainly, Lazarus is dead". (John 11:14)

3. **Hebrews 9:27** And as it is appointed unto men once to die, but after this the judgment:

~~~~~~

God's Life Assurance Plan

If you belong to any of these "Churches of Broad Way" I urge you to seek the truth and repent. God isn't going to allow man to go merrily on his way thinking he can do whatever he wants, worship what ever Gods he feels like, and continually telling lies about Him.

My goal in the writing of this book was to make others aware of the danger of not following God's Word and to seek the truth.

I pray as you read God's Life Assurance Plan, which starts on the next page, that you will realize the promise God has for you, the cost, and how easy it is to become one of God's children, and the result of accepting Jesus and following Him.

If you would like to accept Jesus and you feel it in your heart, won't you pray this prayer right now?

~~~~~~

Dear Lord Jesus,

I accept you as my Savior and Lord of my life. I confess that you are the Son of the Living God. I ask you to forgive me of my sins and take control of the throne of my heart. Make me the kind of person you want me to be.

Amen

~~~~~~

By accepting Jesus as Lord & Savior, you have experienced His love for you. Now you can express your love for Him.

John 14:15 If ye love me, keep my commandments.

Now find a Bible believing church.

The mottoes of my church (The Church of Christ) are:

No book but the Bible.

No creed but the Christ.

No name but the Divine.

No plea but the gospel.

No basis of unity, but the spiritual.

In essentials, unity

In opinions, liberty

In all things, charity

Follow the command to be baptized

Mark 16:16 He that believeth and is baptized shall be saved; but he that believeth not shall be damned.

****

God's Life Assurance Policy

^^^^^^^^^^^^^^

Guaranteed acceptance

Romans 10:13 For whosoever shall call upon the name of the Lord shall be saved

^^^

Rewards after a brief life on Earth

Romans 6:23 For the wages of sin *is* death; but the gift of God *is* eternal life through Jesus Christ our Lord.

^^^

Peace of mind

Romans 8:38-39 For I am persuaded, that neither death, nor life, nor angels, nor principalities, nor powers, nor things present, nor things to come,

39 Nor height, nor depth, nor any other creature, shall be able to separate us from the love of God, which is in Christ Jesus our Lord.

^^^

Immortality

Acts 24:15 And have hope toward God, which they themselves also allow, that there shall be a resurrection of the dead, both of the just and unjust.

^^^

COST

******

Acceptance of the truth

Romans 3:10 As it is written, There is none righteous, no, not one:

Romans 3:23 For all have sinned, and come short of the glory of God;

Romans 5:12 Wherefore, as by one man sin entered into the world, and death by sin; and so death passed upon all men, for that all have sinned:

∧∧

Realize the Price that was paid

Romans 5:8 But God commendeth his love toward us, in that, while we were yet sinners, Christ died for us.

∧∧

Accept Jesus

Romans 10:9-11 That if thou shalt confess with thy mouth the Lord Jesus, and shalt believe in thine heart that God hath raised him from the dead, thou shalt be saved.

10 For with the heart man believeth unto righteousness; and with the mouth confession is made unto salvation.

11 For the Scripture saith, Whosoever believeth on him shall not be ashamed.

Romans 10:13 For whosoever shall call upon the name of the Lord shall be saved.

∧∧

BENEFITS

Luke 13:29 And they shall come from the east, and *from* the west, and from the north, and *from* the south, and shall sit down in the kingdom of God.

Luke 20:35 But they which shall be accounted worthy to obtain that world, and the resurrection from the dead, neither marry, nor are given in marriage:

Luke 20:36 Neither can they die any more: for they are equal unto the angels; and are the children of God, being the children of the resurrection.

Revelation 3:4 Thou hast a few names even in Sardis which have not defiled their garments; and they shall walk with me in white: for they are worthy.

Revelation 7:13-17 And one of the elders answered, saying unto me, What are these which are arrayed in white robes? and whence came they?

14 And I said unto him, Sir, thou knowest. And he said to me, These are they which came out of great tribulation, and have washed their robes, and made them white in the blood of the Lamb.

15 Therefore are they before the throne of God, and serve him day and night in his temple: and he that sitteth on the throne shall dwell among them.

16 They shall hunger no more, neither thirst any more; neither shall the sun light on them, nor any heat.

17 For the Lamb which is in the midst of the throne shall feed them, and shall lead them unto living fountains of waters: and God shall wipe away all tears from their eyes.

Revelation 22:14 Blessed *are* they that do his commandments, that they may have right to the tree of life, and may enter in through the gates into the city.

∧∧

R EFERENCES

Traditions of Men verses The Word of God   By Alvin Jennings

Star Bible Publications, Inc.

Fort Worth, TX.

Churches of Today   by L.G. Tomlinson

Gospel Advocate Company

Nashville, Tenn.

The Random House College Dictionary

201 E., 50th Street

New York, NY. 10022

The History of Apostasies   by John F. Rowe

Old Paths Book Club

Box V

8877 Mission Drive

Rosemead, California

String's Dictionary reference from:

E-Sword, by Rick Meyers

Available on the internet

The Word of God

Author - Our Perpetual, Everlasting God

www.ingramcontent.com/pod-product-compliance
Lightning Source LLC
Chambersburg PA
CBHW020516030426
42337CB00011B/410